Jin's First Day

by Tim Little
Illustrated by Bill Ledger

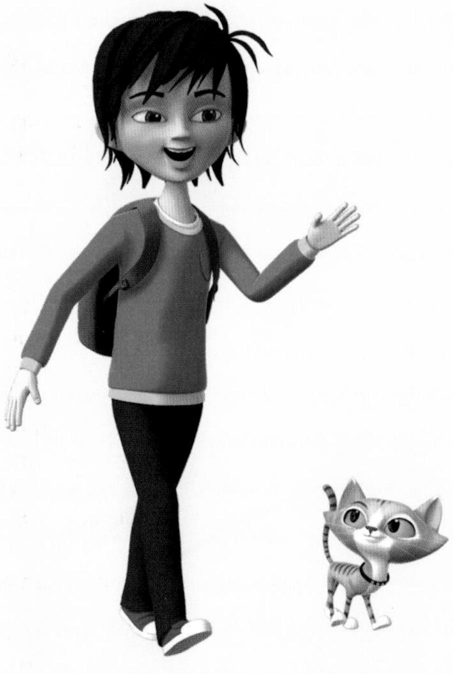

OXFORD
UNIVERSITY PRESS

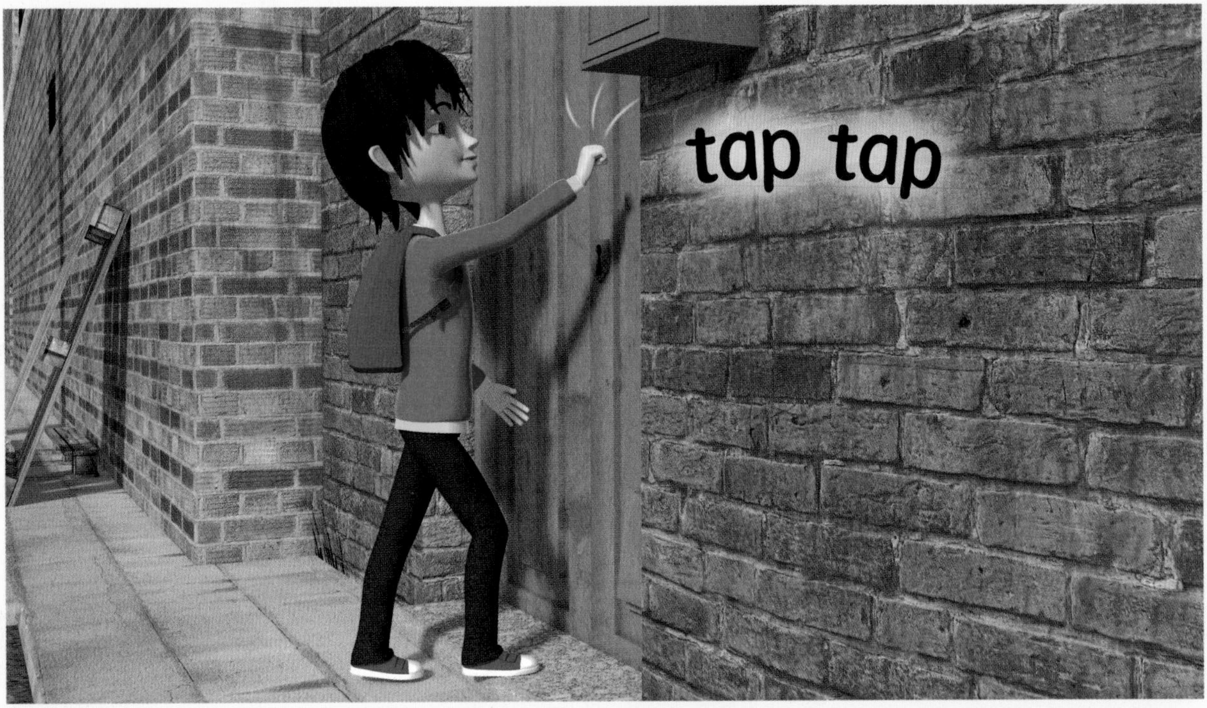
tap tap

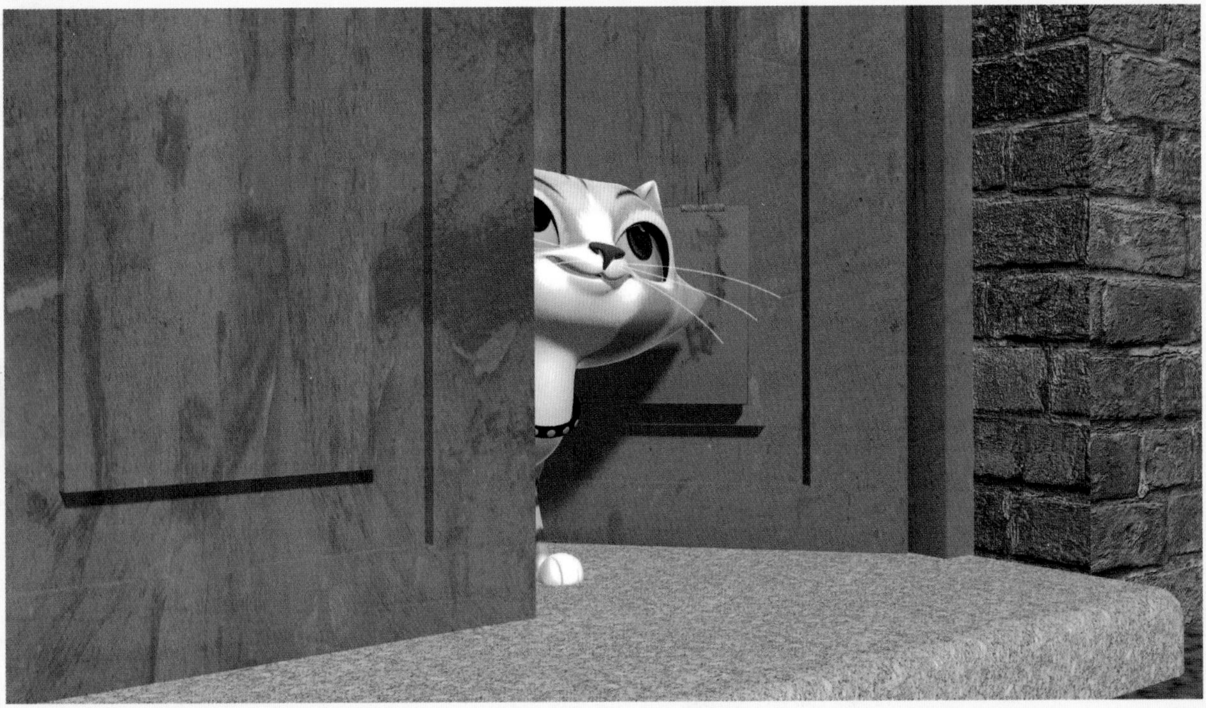

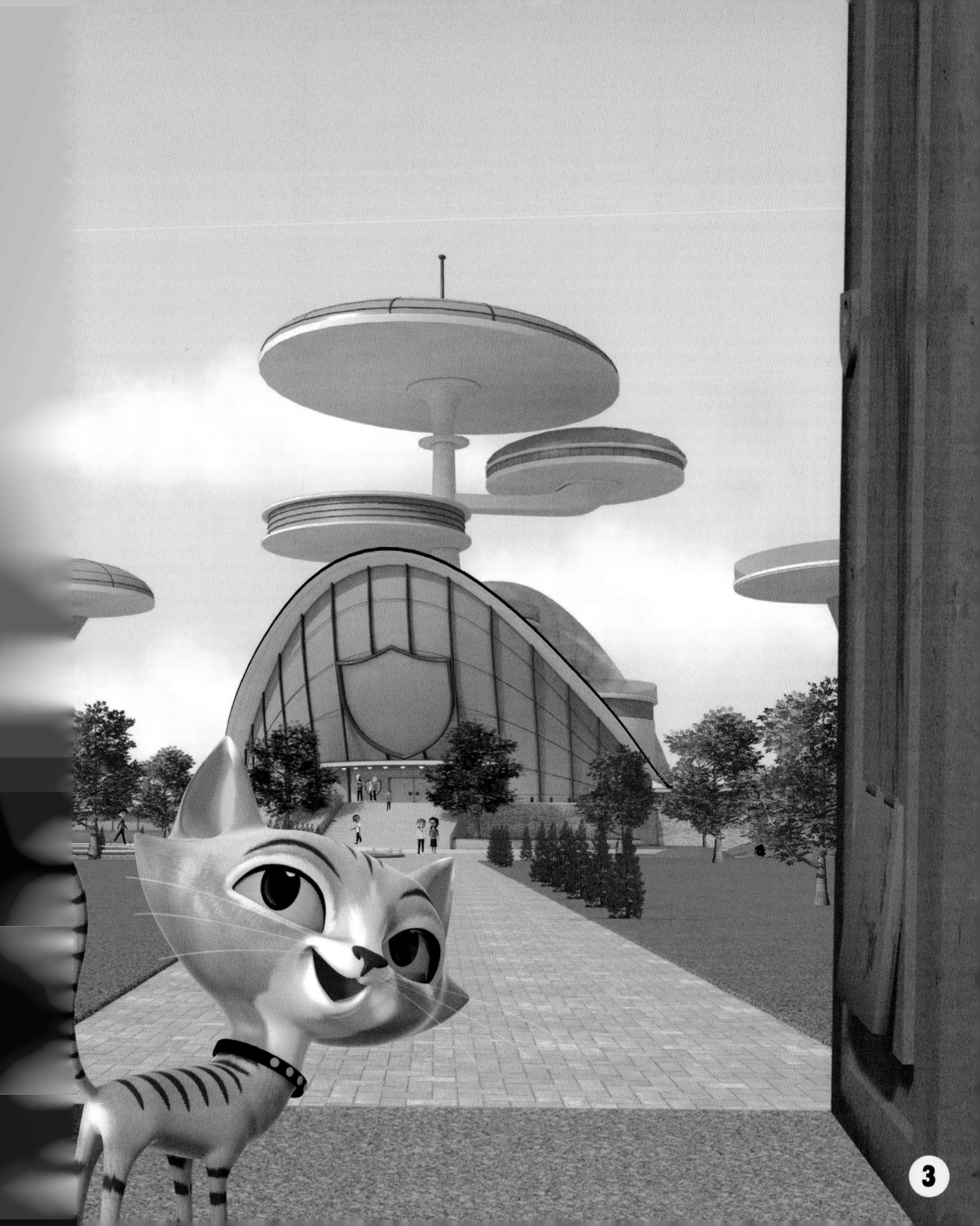

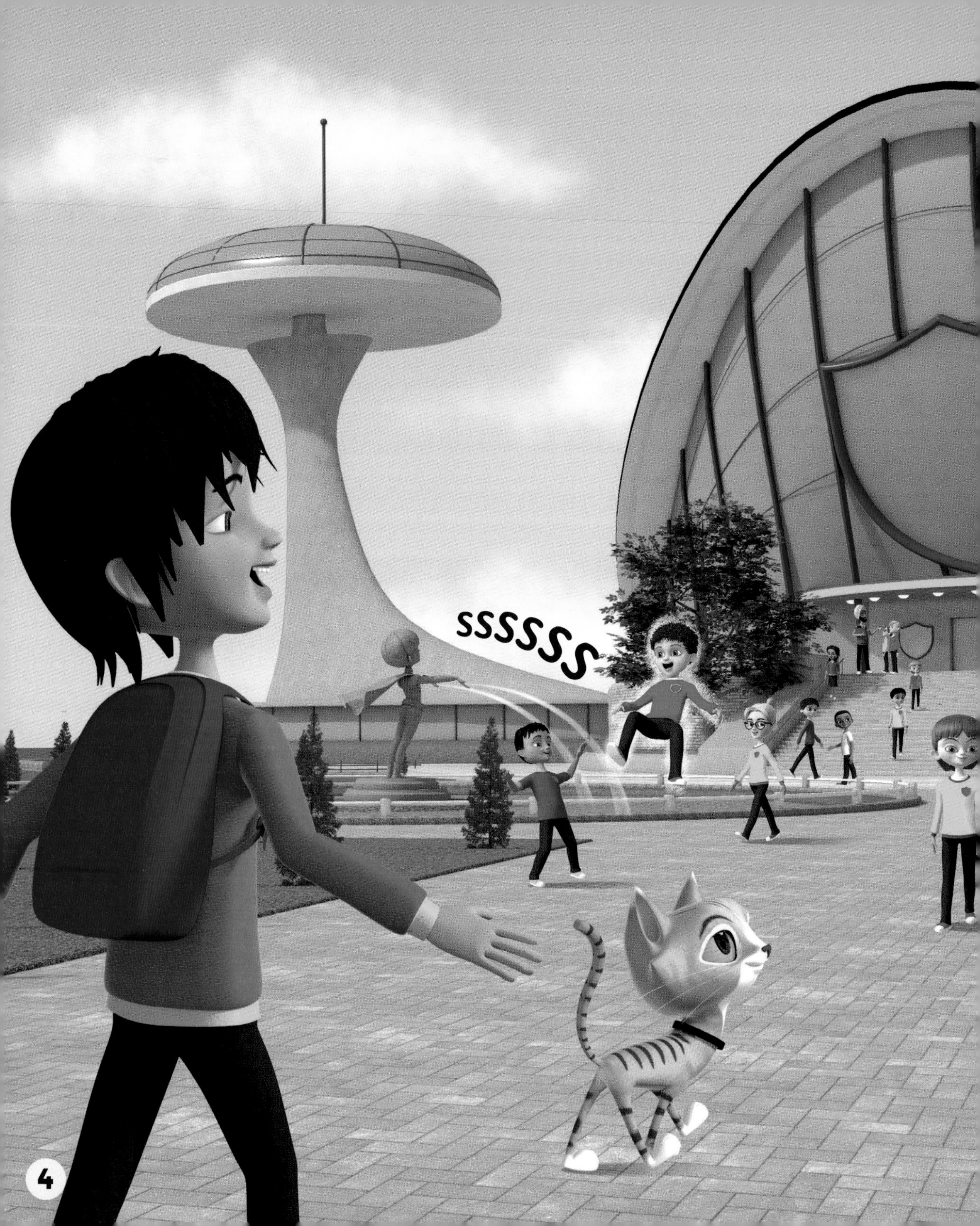
SSSSSS

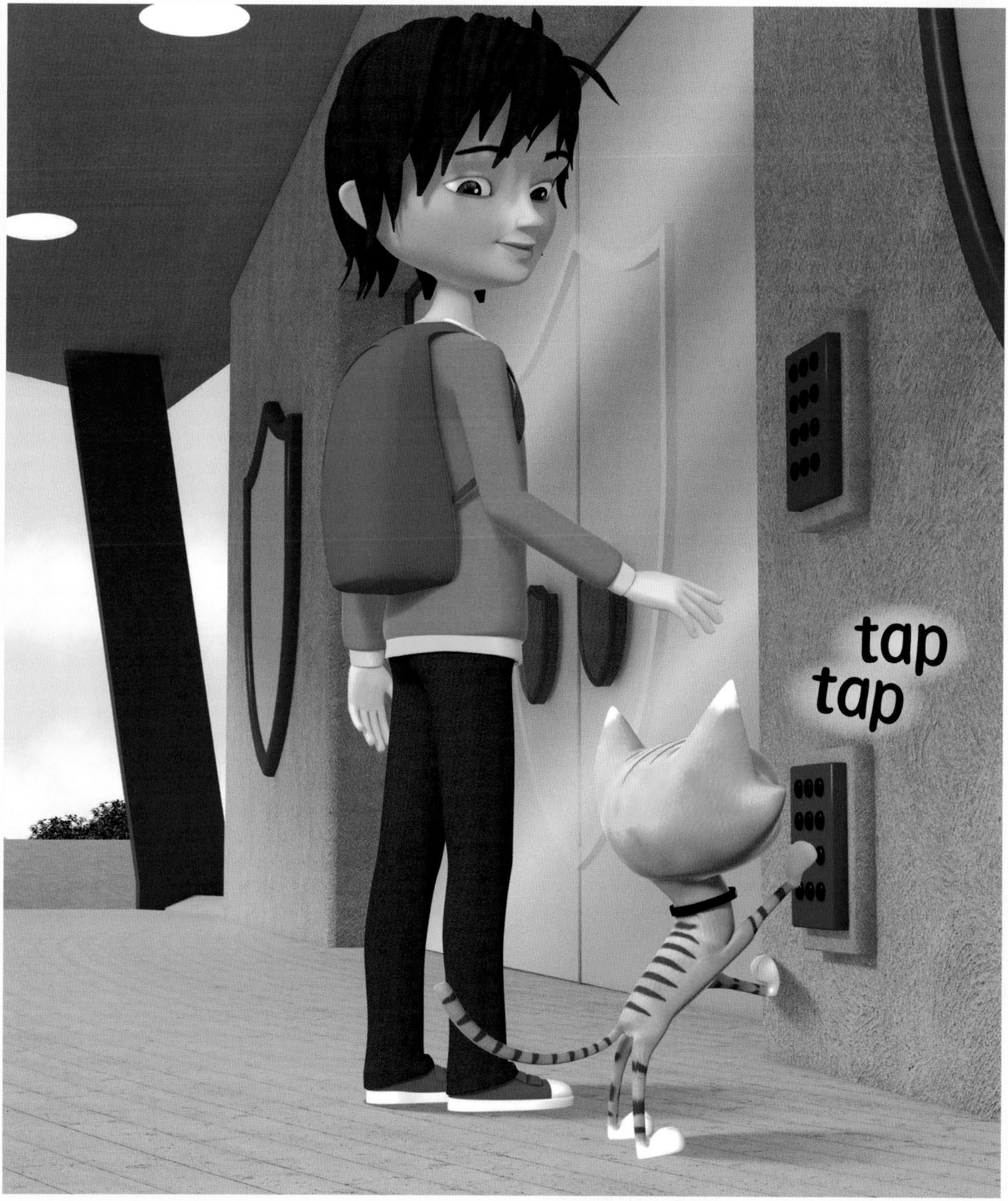
tap
tap

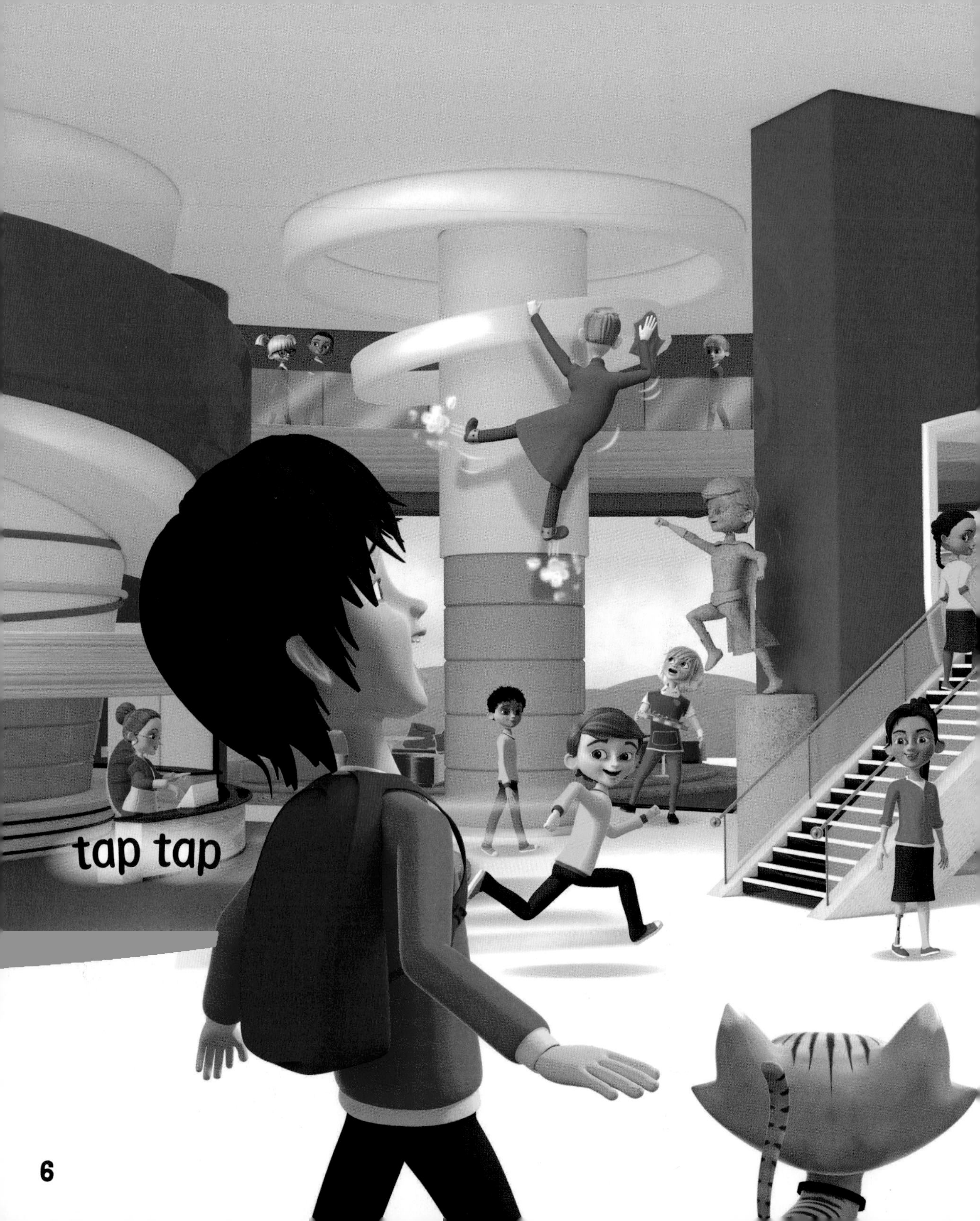
tap tap

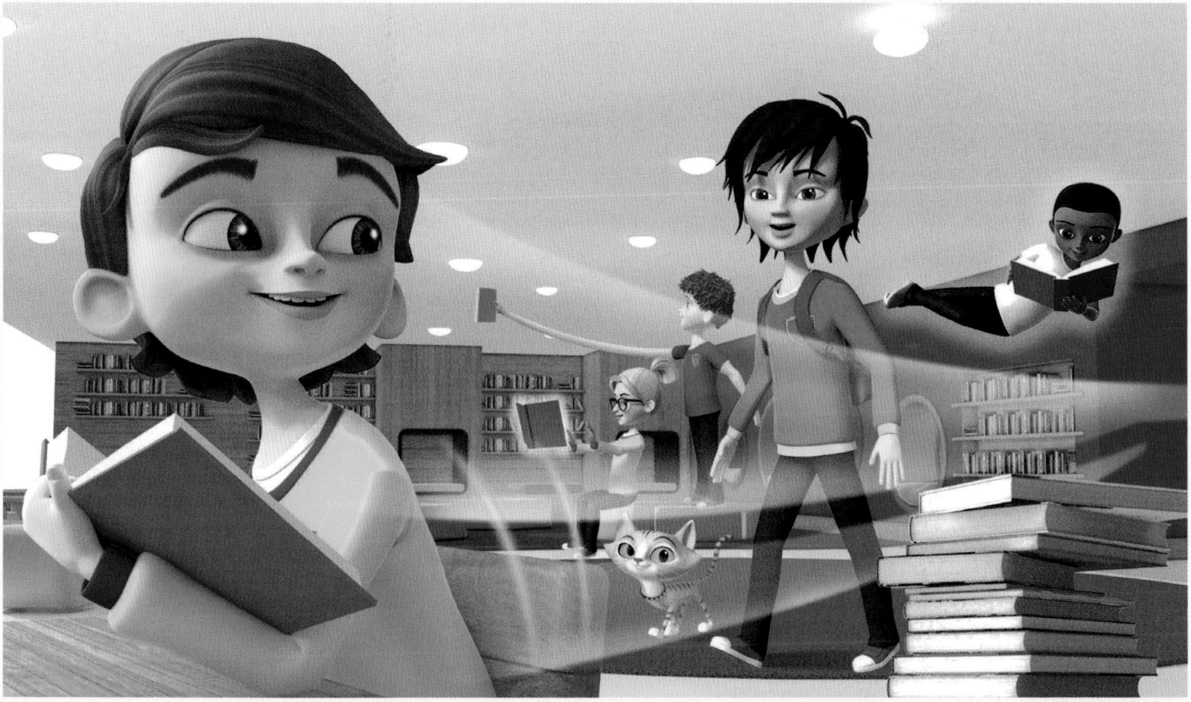

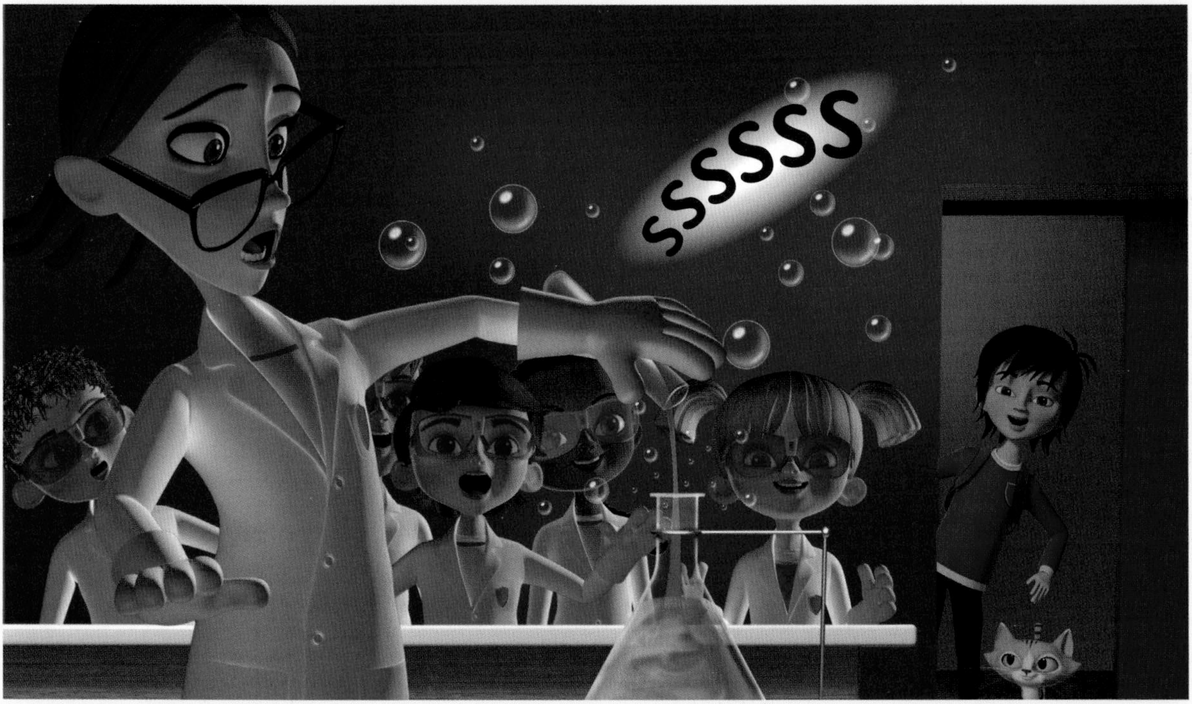
SSSSSS

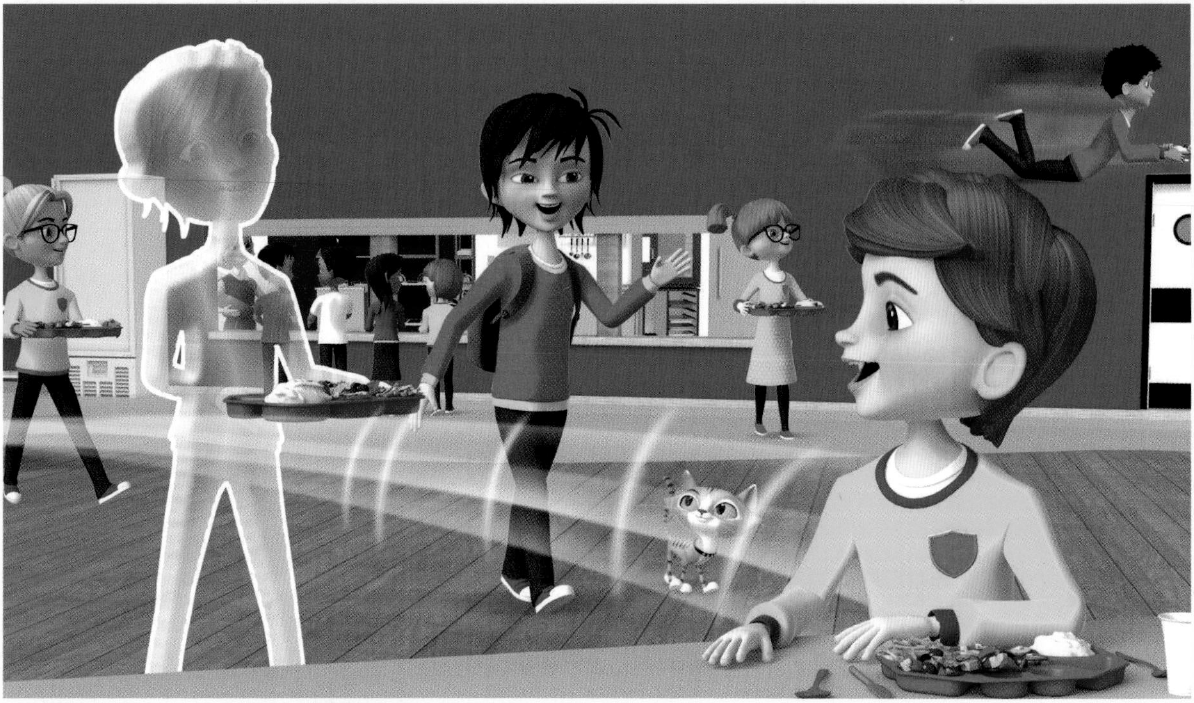

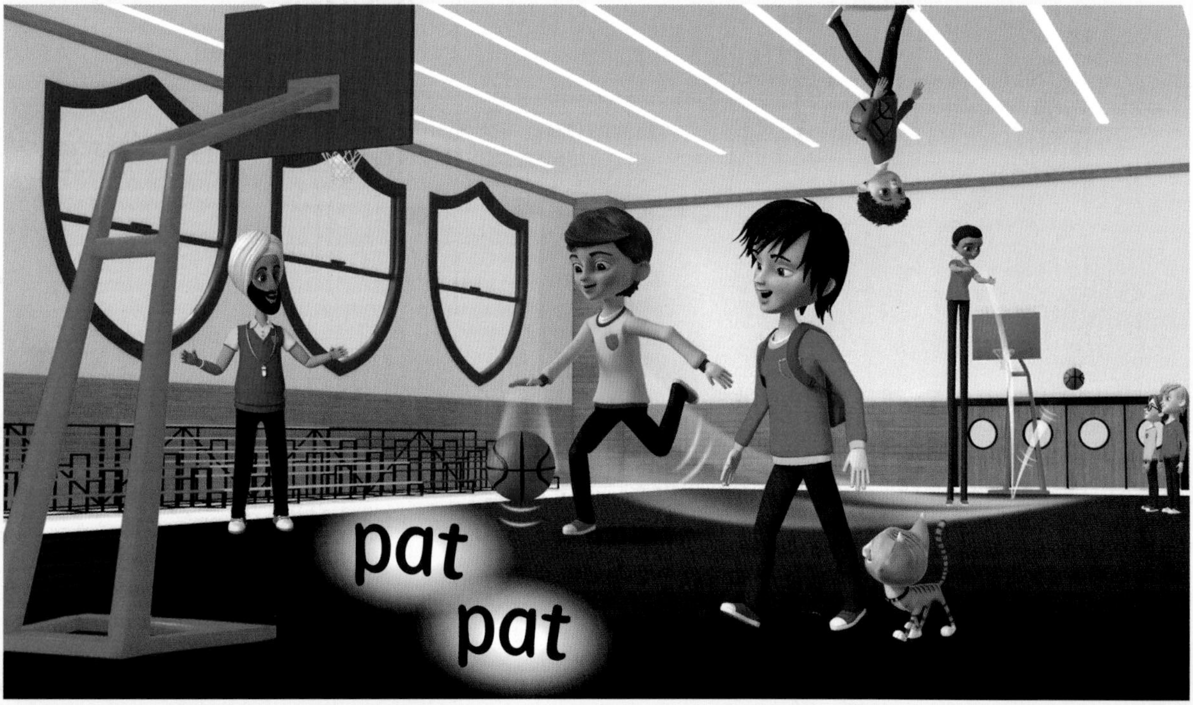
pat
pat

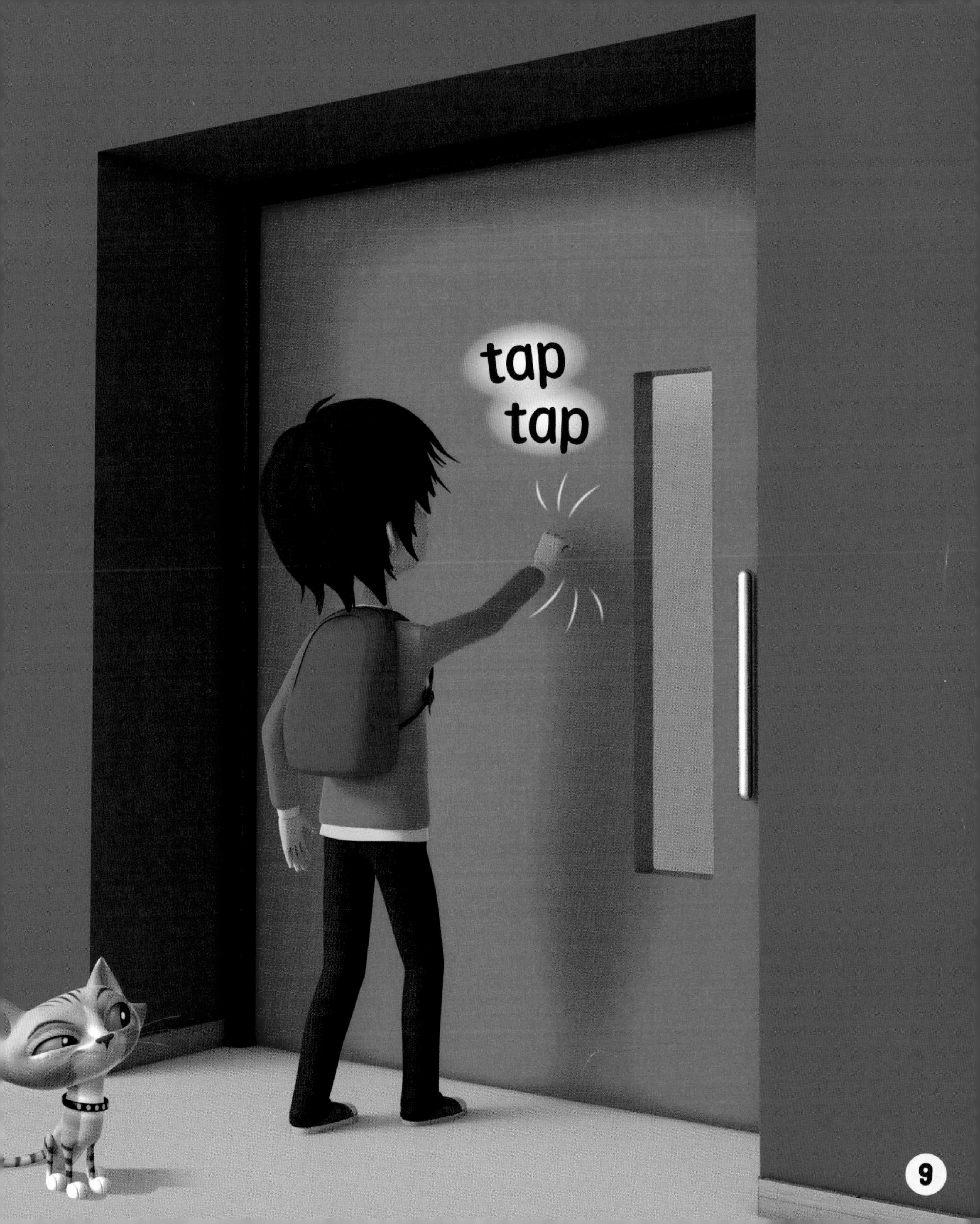
tap
tap

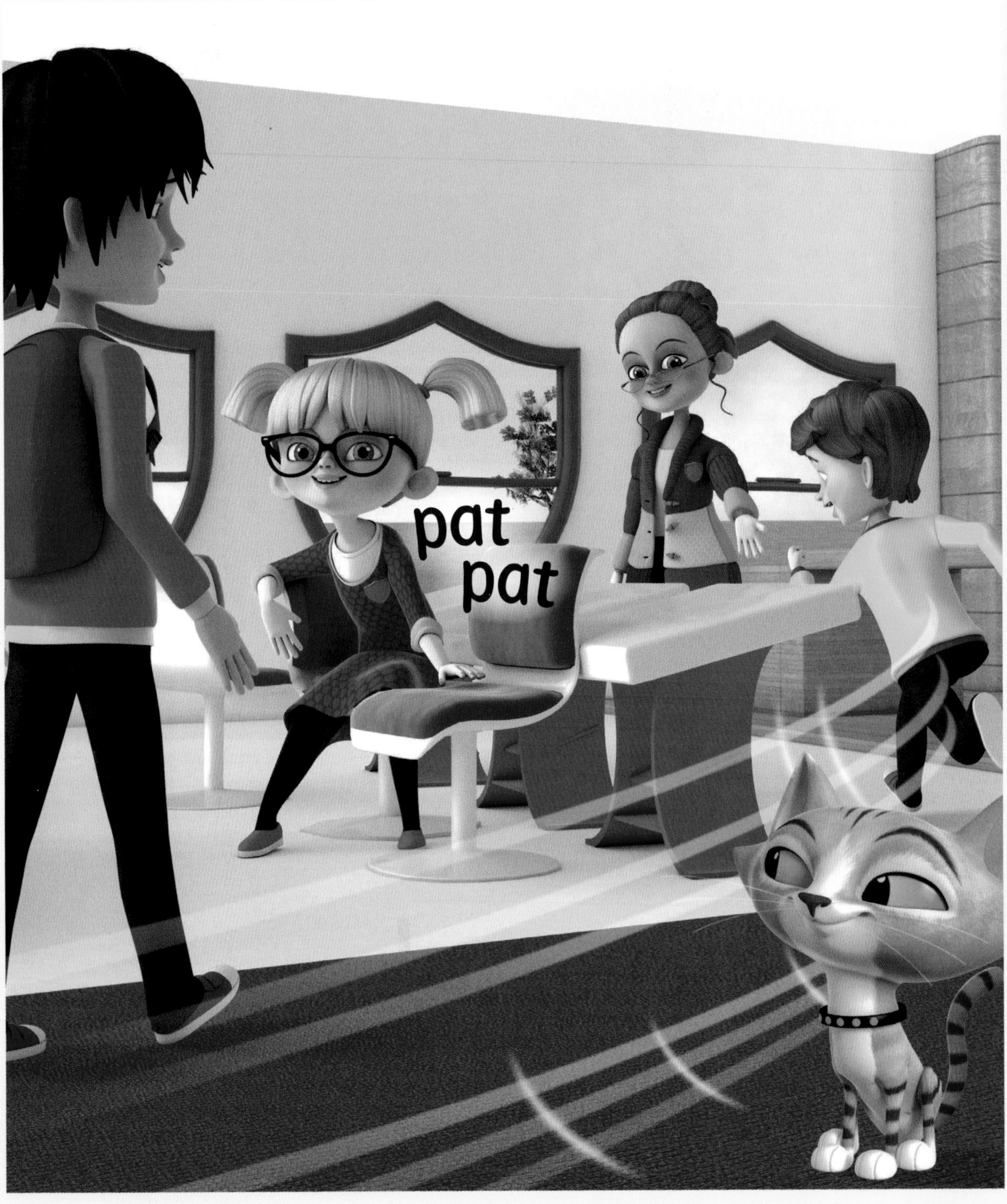
pat
pat

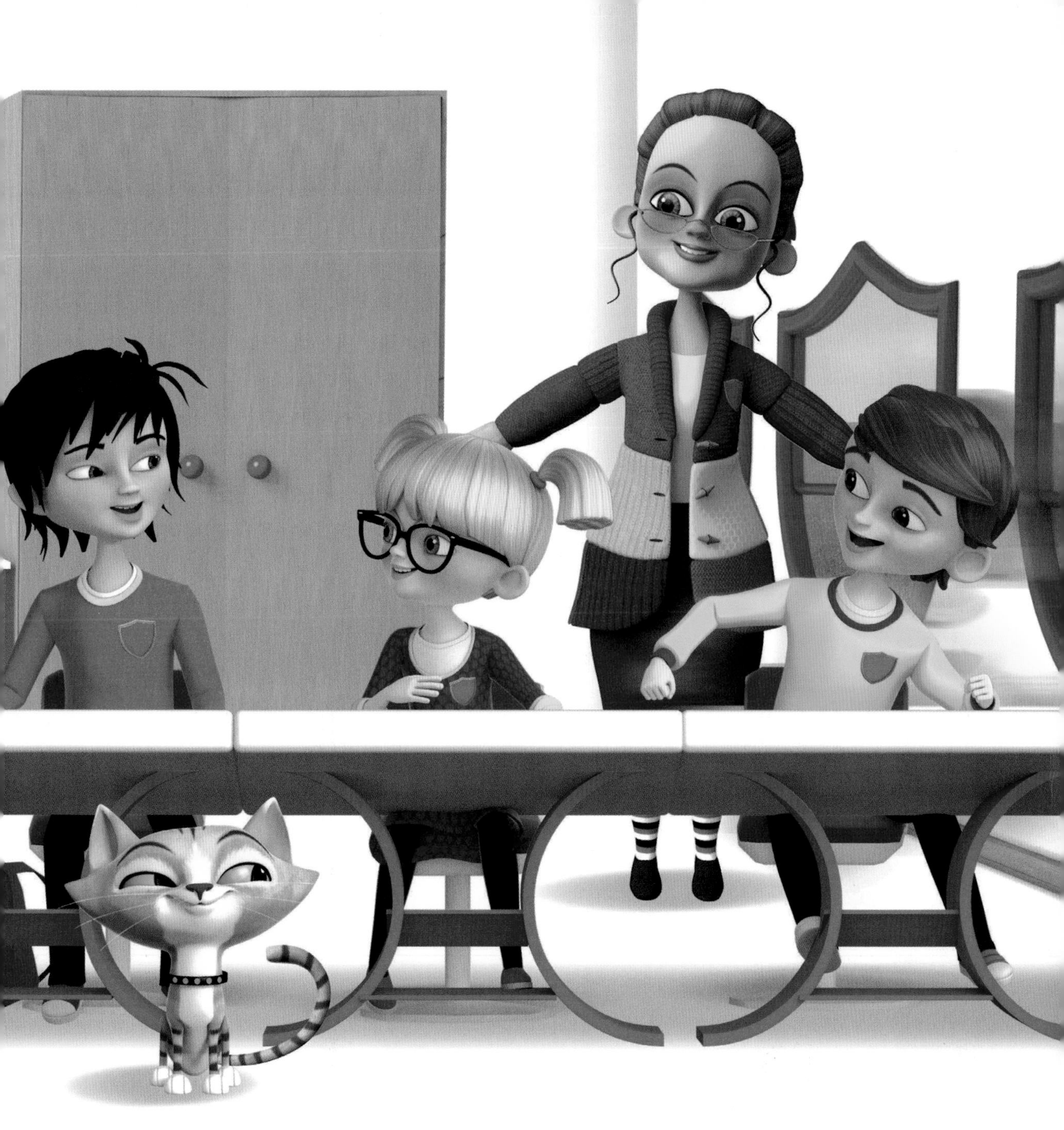

Retell the story ...

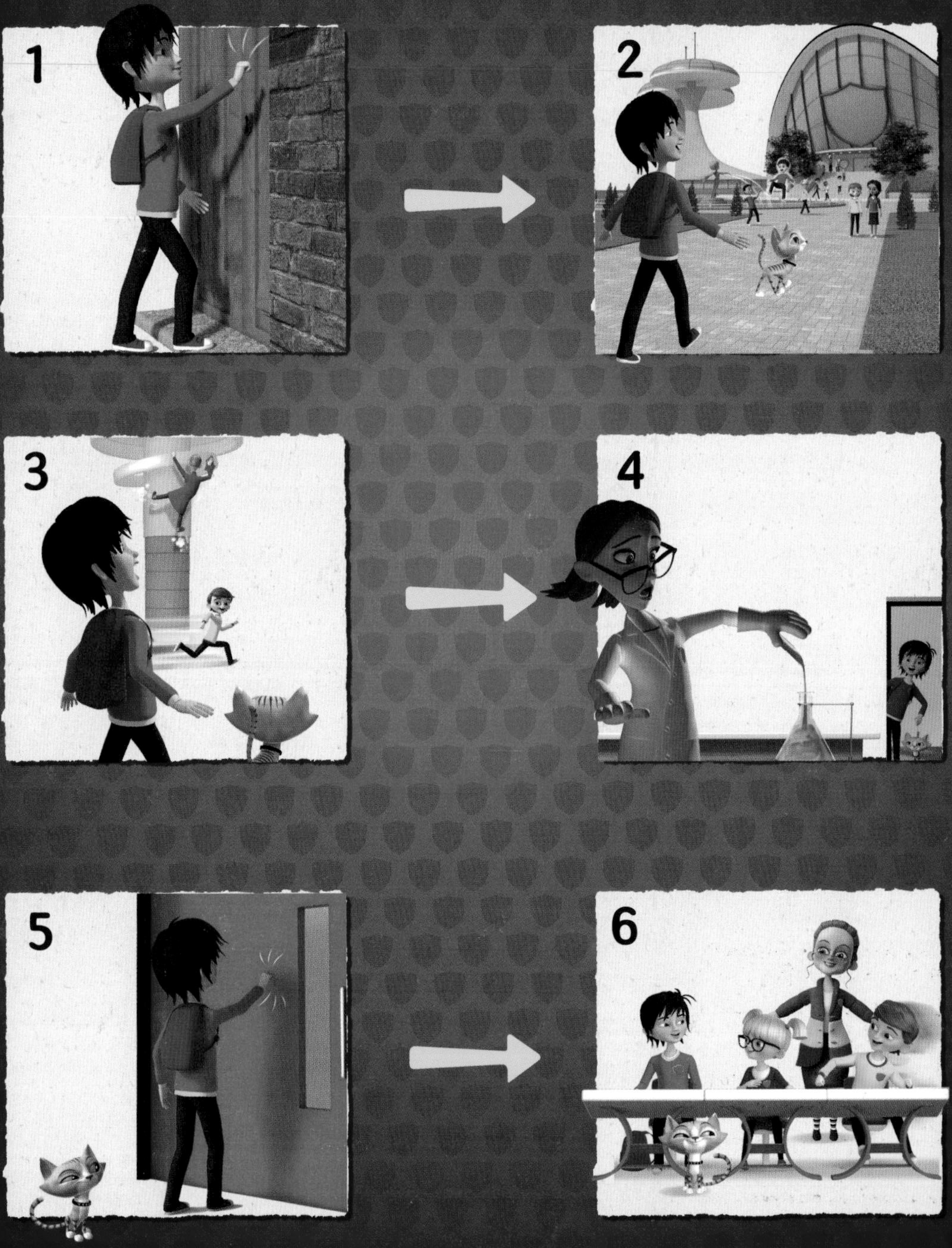